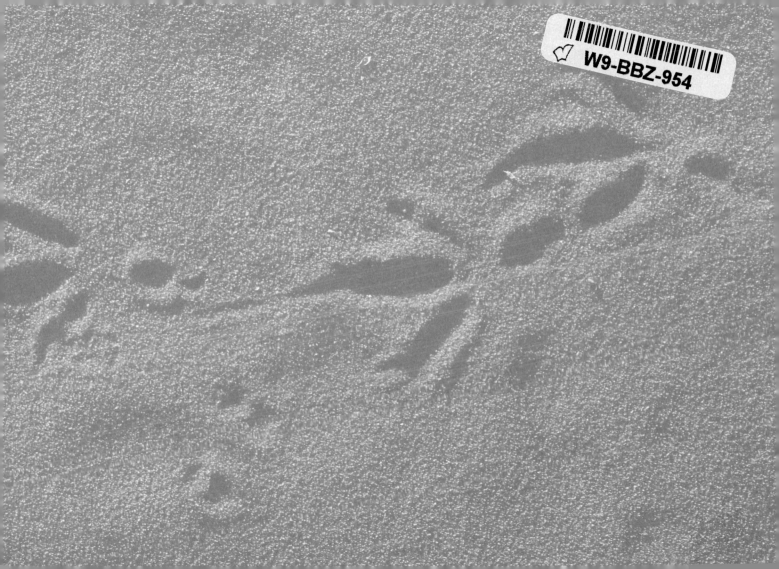

WILDLIFE
AUSTRALIA

PHOTOGRAPHY

PETER LIK & LOCHMAN TRANSPARENCIES

COPYWRITER

ANDREW GRIFFITHS

"My total dedication and obsession
with photography has taken me on
journeys into many remarkable areas
throughout Australia.
I captured much of this collection of
images using a specialist panoramic
camera. Because of the wider field
of view, this format enables me to
portray the true spirit of Australia on
film. Upon viewing these images
I am sure you will share with me the
tranquillity and solitude I experienced
whilst exploring the stunning beauty
of this country."

Telephone: 1300 364 391

CAIRNS
PO Box 2529 Cairns Queensland 4870 Australia
Telephone: (07) 4053 9000   **Fax:** (07) 4032 1277
sales@peterlik.com.au

peterlik.com.au

© **Peter Lik Publishing** BK09
ISBN 0 958 70028 1

Front cover - Koala mother and infant
Back cover - Eastern grey kangaroo joey - 4 months old
Title page - Western pygmy possum feeding on a Grevillea flower

AUSTRALIAN WILDLIFE

Australia is a place of extremes. Within several hundred kilometres you will find snowfields, rainforest, desert, sand dunes and dry eucalypt scrub. To survive in these diverse conditions Australian animals have had to be very adaptable, learning quickly to survive in often harsh and unforgiving environments. They have evolved quickly and spectacularly with the end result being an island filled with birds, mammals, reptiles and insects unlike any other on Earth.

Wildlife Australia has been produced by Peter Lik to introduce some of the well known Australian icons such as the kangaroo, dingo and koala and also to show some of the less well known and harder to find animals like humpback whales, spotted quolls, gecko's and carpet pythons. All of the animals featured in Wildlife Australia are indigenous or native and most can easily be seen in the wild.

Today there is a greater awareness of the importance of protecting native species and their habitat. Wilderness Press is committed to help this process by showcasing Australian wildlife and landscapes in a unique and creative way.

A mother koala and her infant

Koalas are often found sleeping in the fork of eucalypt trees

The koala is considered one of the most unique animals in the world. They can sleep for up to 19 hours per day, only waking to feed on Eucalypt leaves. They are often seen asleep and wedged between the branches of a tall Eucalypt or Gum Tree. Koalas tend to be found in the cooler Eastern parts of Australia. If food is abundant koalas will breed once per year and females can be seen carrying their young on their backs once they have left the pouch.

Koalas walk from tree to tree

Western pygmy possum

Western pygmy possum feeding on a Grevillea flower

Female yellow-bellied sunbird

Chestnut-shouldered fairy-wren found throughout Australia

Hooded parrot common throughout the Northern Territory

Day's frog, Tully, north Queensland

Australia is home to about 200 species of frogs and toads. They are found throughout the country but generally in much higher numbers in warm moist coastal areas. Frogs feed on insects and occasionally other frogs. They do not drink but instead absorb water through their membrane like skin. They also absorb and release gas through their skin.

The white-lipped tree frog is Australia's largest frog

Green and golden bell frog, Eastern Australia

Herbert River ringtail possum and young, North Queensland

Squirrel glider

Dingo fishing in freshwater pool

Dingoes search beaches for anything that may have washed ashore

The dingo is believed to have arrived in Australia with Asian seafarers over 3000 years ago. They are now found throughout Australia, sometimes in large numbers and generally living in packs led by one dominant pair. This pair is often the only one that breeds. Dingoes feed on native animals such as kangaroos and emus. Unfortunately sheep and calves can become a food source in times of drought which makes the dingo a target for graziers and farmers.

Dingo tracks on Fraser Island Queensland

Sooty terns frequent sandy cays on the Great Barrier Reef

Australian gannet female and chick, Shark Bay, Western Australia

Red tailed tropic bird chick on Lady Elliot Island

Southern giant petrel spend most of their life at sea

Mountain brushtail possums

An extremely rare and famous Tasmanian devil family

Wombat

Juvenile numbats in front of burrow

*N*umbats and wombats are mammals which produce milk to feed their young. The numbat is about 25cm long, has a long bushy tail and is only found in south west Australian woodlands. Wombats are closely related to koalas. They are very stong burrowers and are mainly found in the cold southern states.

Common wombats can grow up to 30kg and live in deep burrows

New Zealand fur-seals are found in the colder waters of Southern Australia

An Australian sea-lion pup swims playfully around protective adults

Humpback whale

Australian waters are home to large pods of migrating whales throughout the year. Many species can be seen, including humpback whales, minke whales, killer whales, false killer whales, southern right whales, fin whales, pilot whales and sperm whales. Until 25 years ago whales were hunted around Australia but now boats chasing the whales are filled with people wanting to take photographs. Whale watching has grown to become a large industry in places like Hervey Bay, Queensland.

A diving humpback whale

Why humpback whales breach is uncertain, but it is a very impressive sight

Short beaked echidna looking for ants

Juvenile platypus live in clear freshwater creeks and rivers

Carpet pythons live in urban areas where they eat mice and rats

Soft knob-tailed gecko

Boyd's rainforest dragon feed on fruit and insects

Estuarine crocodiles are common throughout Northern Australia

Northern quoll have sharp teeth and are good hunters

Spotted cuscus, Cape York, Queensland

Herbert River ringtail possum, North Queensland

Australian pelicans can weigh up to 8.2 kg and have a wingspan of 3.4 metres

Pelicans herd fish into shallow water scooping them into their massive bills

Greater bilby

Little red kaluta

Fat-tailed dunnart

An extremely cute Mitchell's hopping mouse

The southern cassowary is flightless and grows to 2 metres in height

If threatened, emus can run at speeds of up to 50 km per hour

Emus are found throughout mainland Australia

An eastern grey kangaroo joey

The common wallaroo has characteristics of wallabies and kangaroos

Eastern grey kangaroo with a joey in the pouch

Kangaroos, wallabies and wallaroos make up a group of animals called Macropods, which in Greek means "big footed". They are abundant throughout mainland Australia and Tasmania. Macropods are without doubt the most well known of the Australian animals. They are herbivores and their numbers fluctuate according to the supply of food available. Kangaroos have adapted to the harsh Australian climate by reproducing in great numbers in times of plenty and in times of drought females can stop ovulating altogether.

Eastern grey kangaroos blend with the harsh Australian bush

Eastern grey kangaroo on the hop

Even though Australia is considered a very dry continent there are vast Wetland areas, lakes and river systems that are home for hundreds of species of water birds. Being the only real land mass between South America and Africa makes Australia the perfect stopover for migrating birds. Seasonal climatic changes, particularly in the Northern parts of Australia, change dry rivers into flood plains overnight. With the rain comes the water birds who feed until the water dries up and they are forced to move on.

Pacific black ducks live in large large lakes and wetland areas

Seasonal wetlands provide abundant food for water birds

Black swans have a wingspan up to 2 metres

The frilled lizard uses it scary appearance to warn off predators

Although fearsome looking, the thorny devil lizard has an extremely placid nature

Lesser wanderer butterfly drinking from a dew drop

Pale green triangle butterfly, North Queensland

Green spotted triangle butterfly, North Queensland

The magnificent sight of a swarm of wanderer butterflies

Flocks of budgerigars can sometimes number over ten thousand birds

A mating pair of electus parrots at the nest

Pink cockatoo at the nest entrance

Little penguins, known as fairy penguins, are the smallest of all penguins

Macaroni penguin colony provides safety in numbers

Kingfishers are common throughout mainland Australia. The most well known of the species is the laughing kookaburra. All kingfishers are aggressive hunters with the larger birds such as kookaburras killing snakes and goannas. Some kingfishers live in hollowed out termite mounds which make perfect nests. Kingfishers tend to have dazzling neon coloured plumage making them popular with bird watching enthusiasts.

Forest kingfisher found throughout Australasia

A white-tailed kingfisher flying from a nest in a termite mound

Blue winged kookaburra

Bottlenose dolphins frequently investigate boats and swimmers

Dugong swimming above coral reef

Wetlands at sunset

The very graceful large egret

Jabiru, Australia's only native stork

The fearsome looks of a wedge tailed eagle

The southern boobook owl feeds on mice, sparrows and large insects

Western swamp tortoise

Green turtles are common along the Great Barrier Reef

Turtle tracks indicate a female has come ashore to lay her eggs

A green turtle coming ashore to lay eggs

White-breasted sea eagle juvenile in flight

Hawk catching fish

Whistling kite perched at sunset

Peter Lik Galleries

Lik's original design concept was to create a contemporary space that enhances the natural beauty of his imagery, and the galleries continue to evolve under his direction. Attracting a diverse mix of visitors and collectors, the galleries are a fitting environment in which to experience an extraordinary photographic collection.

Each gallery offers the highest level of framing professionalism available and fully insures each piece, delivered to your doorstep worldwide.

A team of experienced Art Consultants are on hand to guide the visitor through their journey, or they can simply relax and enjoy the gallery at their leisure.

CAIRNS
4 Shields Street
Cairns Qld 4870 Australia
Telephone [07] 4031 8177
cairns@peterlik.com.au

LAHAINA
712 Front Street
Maui, Hawaii 96761 USA
Telephone [808] 661 6623
lahaina@peterlik.com

LAS VEGAS
Forum Shops at Caesars
3500 Las Vegas Blvd South
Las Vegas NV 89109 USA
Telephone [702] 836 3310
lasvegas@peterlik.com

NOOSA
Shop 2, Seahaven 9 Hastings Street
Noosa Heads Qld 4567 Australia
Telephone [07] 5474 8233
noosa@peterlik.com.au

PORT DOUGLAS
19 Macrossan Street
Port Douglas Qld 4871 Australia
Telephone [07] 4099 6050
port@peterlik.com.au

SYDNEY
Level 2 QVB
455 George Street Sydney
NSW 2000 Australia
Telephone [02] 9269 0182
sydney@peterlik.com.au

peterlik.com

Books by Peter Lik

LARGE FORMAT PUBLICATIONS